THE WAY OF THE CROSS

IN

SANTA MARIA, CA.

THE WAY OF THE CROSS

IN

SANTA MARIA, CA.

RENE LAURENTIN

TRANSLATED BY

SUZANNE SHUTTE   HOUSTON , TEXAS
ANIK ALVAREZ   SANTA MARIA, CA.
FRANCOIS NIELSON   SAN LOUIS OBISPO, CA.

Queenship
PUBLISHING COMPANY
Santa Barbara, California

ABOUT THE COVER

On April 19, 1988, Carol Nole received through an inner locution from the Blessed Virgin Mary, important elements pertaining to the design of the Cross she wants erected overlooking the Santa Maria Valley in California. Our Lady specified the Cross to be seventy five feet high, with a proportional crossbeam. It will have one foot holes with golden stained glass where the nails were, rather than a corpus. *(A Cross will Be Built ... p. 3.)*

In December 1988 a seven month project fabricating a scale model of the Cross was completed by Patrick Shelton and Mackey Real of Santa Maria. During the preliminary planning phase the Blessed Mother gave an inner locution to Carol on May 23, 1988 affirming the design:

"... My children, my Son is pleased with your design. The boldness, strength, beauty and grace are combined with the most important, love from your heart. It reaches out to all My Children..." *(A Cross will Be Built ... p.4)*

The model of the Cross, constructed of stainless steel, select woods and stained glass, is exhibited in the Regional Bishop's office in Santa Barbara, California. Photography for the cover of Fr. Laurentin's book was done by Wm Dewey Studio of Santa Barbara.

Publisher's Foreword

This book is a account of Fr. Laurentin's investigations and his trips to Santa Maria, California.

The two parts of this book where originally written to appear in *Stella Maris* a periodical published quarterly in Europe in French and German. These two articles will appear in two separate editions in 1993. Father Laurentin is a regular contributor to *Stella Maris*.

Since both articles concern the United States and Santa Maria, California, we have, with Fathers Laurentin's permission, combined them into one book.

About Father Laurentin

René Laurentin was born in Tours, France, October 19, 1917 of Maurice Laurentin, an architect, and of Mary Jactel. He did his secondary (high school) studies at St. Mary of Cholet Institute and entered the Seminary of Carmes, at the Catholic Institute of Paris in

October 1934. He obtained two Masters Degrees, in Philosophy and Thomistic Philosophy at the Sorbonne (1938)

At the end of his first year of Theology (1937-1938) he did his military service as an Infantry Officer during World War II. He was decorated with the Military Cross, two citations and the Legion of Honor. He was taken prisoner in Belgium (May 1940) and spent five years as a German prisoner. After the war (1945) he returned to his studies, receiving his degree in Theology in July 1946. He was ordained to the priesthood in the sasme year on December 8th. Fr. Laurentin prepared three theses on the Virgin Mary as part of his Masters work. In 1952 he received his Doctor of Philosophy Degree from the Sorbonne with highest honors for two thesis on the Motherhood of Mary: one historical and the other Iconographical. He acquired his Doctor of Theology Degree, Cum Laude in 1953.

Some of his accomplishments include:

- Professor of Theology at the Catholic University Angers 1953
- Member of the International Marian Academy of Rome 1955
- Vice President of the French Society of Marian studies 1962
- Consultant to the preparatory commissions of Vatican II in 1960
- Expert of the Vatican II Council from 1962 to 1965
- Member of three Mariological Academies in Rome
- Member of the Pontifical Theological Academy of Rome
- Currently a Visiting Professon, University of Dayton, Ohio and the Pontifical Catechatical Institute of Arlington, Va.

In addition Father Laurentin had written over 100 books by 1989 (many more by 1993). He has written over 1,500 articles, many of which have been published world wide. He has also participated in numerous radio and television broadcasts, not only in France, but throughout Europe, and North and South America. He has also found time to participate in many conferences, meetings etc..

Aware that theology demands a liturgical life and profound prayer, he practices a pastoral ministry in a contemplative convent in the suburbs of Paris.

The Publisher
February 1993

PART I

THE GRACES AND TRIALS

Humble Prayers from the Middle Class of Sanctity

In July and August of 1991 and again in September of 1992 I visited the apparition sites of the American Far West, beginning in Santa Maria, California: 64,000 people, located about 130 miles north of Los Angeles.

The Virgin has told the seers that she is asking for the erection of a Cross on the top of a hill. A great impetus of prayer and generosity has welcomed her request but

1

the land owners refuse to budge and give up the land.

This is not the first time she has asked. In 1848 St. Catherine Laboure, seer of the Miraculous Medal, was asked by Our Lady to erect a large Cross overlooking Paris. She was not able to secure it because of a refusal by diocesan authorities. (R. Laurentin, Vie de Catherine Laboure). The same refusal came from church authority in erecting a Cross asked for in Dozule, in Normandy. The height of the Dozule Cross, 738 meters, caused fear. The seer Madeline, was obedient and discrete but did not make it clear enough that the number (738) was symbolic: the altitude of Jerusalem. These apparitions are frequently an occasion of tensions and misunderstandings. This is my daily life of discernments.

My Arrival in Santa Maria

In July 1991, my friends Doris and Ernesto Laguette, contacted me in Medjugorje one night between eleven and midnight to persuade me to come to Santa Maria. In the end I accepted their invitation.

After my arrival in California, we traveled along the Pacific Coast to Santa Maria for a meeting with Carol Nole who had received the message and a fervent group who took to heart the erection of this Cross. A discrete meeting I thought, because I always have a fear that requires a guarantee of "caution" when meeting any seer.

I wanted to go there very peacefully, thinking I would meet Carol and the people at her home. I was surprised to discover 1,600 people in a large gymnasium. They were waiting for my attendance at an hour long conference with a Mass and homily in English: I was unaware of this until just before I arrived. I only thought I would join in their prayers and celebration. I found their lovely popular devotion to be generous, united and inspiring with a confident peace in listening to God.

The friends of the Cross joyfully meet three times on the week end for 16 hours of prayer:

7:00 P. M. to 9:30 P. M. on Fridays
11:00 A. M. to 7:00 P. M. on Saturday, with the Rosary and testimonies (and a break for food). The schedule is the same on Sundays.

Carol Nole, who received the message from Our Lady, is there at the entrance of the gymnasium, a long line waits for her counsel. She is a young grandmother (in her fifties) with a thin, aesthetic, smiling face. Her welcome is attentive, happy and very humble. She is devoted to counseling and giving spiritual advice to a diversified group of people, as the gathering is by in large a mix of cultures. She gives priority to the poor, the sick and the afflicted: extending a friendly welcome inspired with the same maternal concern as the Blessed Mother. She shows much humility and states precisely:

I am neither a priest nor a doctor or a psychologist. Go to specialists for specific problems. I can only pray for you and be with you.

Her presence and counseling is appreciated very much.

1. CAROL'S CROSS TO BEAR

Carol Nole has gone through a difficult life. She has three children and has been divorced. The Church recognized the nullity of her first marriage and she was re-married to Charlie Nole who has 7 children. He has also been divorced and obtained an annulment from the Church. Their respective children are adults and living their own way of life.

An Appeal of Our Lady

On March 24, 1988, she surprisingly received a rush of spiritual joy!

You will be my messenger.

Was this an intuition, an inspiration or a locution? I asked her in distinct terms.

I received it word for word!

Have you had similar experiences before?

Never.

April 9 she receives this announcement.

A Cross will be built on the north side of town on the hill directly in line with the back of Scolari's market...It will be 75 feet in height (equal to 25 meters)...It will have golden stained glass where the nail holes were. It must radiate love and peace over your valley.

She carefully noted each message: Her locutions (words) were not accompanied by visions or apparitions.

Discovery of the Hill

On April 25 Carol received the directions for discovering the place chosen according to the indications of Our Lady. This really put her insight to the test because the site finally identified was not so visible from Scolari's market. The site is not a summit but rather a hill in a small valley located quite low among the other hills. One can access it by highway 166 that winds through the area located between Bakersfield and Santa Maria.

Carol received this announcement:

Let those who want, participate with no glory, except in doing my Son's work.

The group is very welcoming, they do not discriminate against any culture, social status or ethnic background. One can find beautiful Indians and Asians who come there.

The messages that follow are an invitation to the spiritual life: becoming aware of the love of Christ and entering in without reserve. They are short and stop September 2, 1988. They were received in less than 6 months and fill less than 5 pages. They were printed in March of 1989 in a small booklet totaling 10 pages with an introduction and the necessary disclaimers.

First Pilgrimages

The people of Santa Maria gathered by word of mouth. By April 28, 1989 there were 60 visitors at the site of the future Cross. Following on May 5: 125 visitors climbed the hill to see the rock Cross that had been formed on the ground (which is useless for cultivation). Then the crowds increased. The foreman of the ranch, employed by Newhall Land and Farming Company, (23823 Valencia Blvd., Valencia, Ca) passed by on horseback. He spoke with the first pilgrims but did not object to them being there.

No "Trespassing" by the Owners

But soon after, the foreman of the ranch referred the matter to the company's administrative headquarters. The reaction was prompt and they posted signs near the fence: *"Do not enter or you will be prosecuted."* The pilgrims were obedient as they were not fanatics. On May 29 there were 250 people on the site but they remained on the other side of the road on a small bluff several feet wide. They were able to view the hill from across the road but were separated from the property by the fence which no one has crossed since.

The foreman then notified the County Sheriff who sent eight Deputies to investigate. They observed the good order and reported back to their superior. However, Sheriff became concerned because the gatherings alongside the highway were causing unacceptable risks for the pilgrims. He notified a highway department official who said he would need to forbid the gatherings unless protective barriers were installed. The group could not afford the cost of the barriers (sixteen thousand dollars).

The signs that mandate "no trespassing" are periodically replaced by ones bearing greater actions of compliance. The last ones I photographed on September 1, 1992 said:

Danger Cattle Grazing
Rocky Terrain Snakes
No Trespassing
Violators Will be Prosecuted

The friends of the Cross were obedient. On June 25, 1990 they came in mass for the last time: every hour on the hour but in small groups. They had been able to pray on the side of the road for a long time without reprisals. A professional gardener named Greg was inspired to plant rose bushes on the side of the road but the foreman pulled the plants out of the ground and posted a prohibition of planting bushes between the embankment and the fence.

After this, the decisions of the foreman were accepted with patience and discipline. The stones that the first pilgrims had aligned on the ground in the form of a Cross also had to be destroyed and scattered. The supporters of the project accepted this desecration without a word.

Charlie Nole, Carol's husband, was the group's spokesman. He is said to have a brilliant experience in business affairs and has quit his job in order to serve Our Lady's project. It was from the foreman that he learned that the rock Cross (on top of the hill) had been destroyed (because no one was allowed to go up on the forbidden hill).

He courteously pursued the negotiations with the Newhall Farming Company but without success. They did not want to sell the barren piece of land. They wanted to keep it reserved for their own future projects. The corporate administrator stood by the company directive and defended their rights.

The negotiations intensified on all fronts. Besides Charlie, a protestant church and another individual had offered to buy the land from the farming company . They wanted to donate the land to the Cross of Peace Corporation for the realization of the project. This only exasperated the owners and made them more nervous. They multiplied their complaints and stood their ground. They sent reports to the civil authorities about the dangers of people gathering near their property; they wrote the Archbishop of Los Angeles asking him to quiet his "straying sheep" and demanded that he establish "good order."

The Cardinal was in no hurry. Santa Maria is located in his huge diocese (Santa Barbara, Pastoral Region) but the site for the Cross is located in another diocese (Monterey). He would not hear of engaging himself in this affair and left it in the care of responsible local authority according to principles established at the Vatican Council II: The higher ranking authority must avoid substituting itself for the lesser ranking authority when the latter is able to take care of its own responsibilities.

Since the group was not allowed to pray at the site chosen by Our Lady, in September of 1992 they asked the locutionist (Carol Nole) if the project could be temporarily be transferred to another location in this vast region of uncultivated hills. *"No, the project is not to be transferred,"* said her husband Charlie: *"The Virgin seems to have given us the assurance that eventually all of the difficulties will be resolved one day."*

2. DISCERNMENT

What Is to Be Thought of the Multiplication of Seers?

I don't have authority to pass judgement and in any case, final discernment is exercised on a level where even Episcopal or Papal authority are cautious. So much of this is complex.

Briefly, prayer is communication with God and the Holy Spirit, who normally gives to every serious Christian illuminations, inspirations, or movements which guide, elevate and transform one's spiritual activities. For some Christians, this communication is received in a more appreciable form: locutions, interior visions or apparitions. These more particular favors are not necessarily an indication of great holiness. They adapt to the disposition of each person's natural perceptions, imagination and psychic capacities. It is difficult to say in what measure these apparent phenomena are the effect of a special extraordinary action or a miracle of God.

The important thing is the authenticity of the communication and of its fruits: conversions and healings. Whether the communication is either miraculous or discrete matters very little. The most hidden is often the most profound. In Santa Maria the prayer is fervent and the fruits are evident. The people are thankful. This fervor is often put to the test in these vibrant and ardent communities by the frequency of phenomenon as in the times of St. Paul in Corinth: wherever the charisms awaken they are often abounding and unequally convincing. When the charisms become a topic of discussion they can create divisions. How should one discern?

3. The Other Seers

My hosts arranged for me to meet with several people who had come to Santa Maria and experienced visions or locutions. I met with some of them in a motorhome in the parking lot near the place of prayer at Alan Hancock College on July 26-27, 1991.

JUAN DIAZ

Juan, a young man (26 years old), pleasant and well balanced told me about his fruitful experience:

In March of 1990 we went to the side of the road near the hill to pray. There were about 40 of us and we all saw the Virgin: with a long white veil. She was standing on some sort of cloud. I also saw Christ crowned with thorns and I began to pray in tongues.

Do you belong to a charismatic prayer group? I asked him.

No.

Did you know what praying in tongues was?

Somewhat. The others also prayed in tongues. When I saw the Virgin I wished that I could have died in order to stay with her. She was surprised that I did not share this experience with the others. Then I did tell my prayer group (in his home town) about my experience and I saw her a second time.

Do you still wish you could die?

Yes, to be with her, but I understood that she needed my work here so I decided it would be better not to die. I have contacted the Claretians to enter their Dominguez Seminary near Los Angeles.

Are you entering in September? (1991)

I am debating because I have established a prayer group and I might take a year for reflection and to remain with the group.

Even if the visions of this young man present peculiarities at first glance, the fruits are good. His humility as well as his decisions speak in his favor. In September of 1992 Monsignor Rohde was told that Juan had entered the Claretian seminary.

PAUL

Another seer takes us further, in a more touching way; in the heart of poverty: in a servant's position. Paul is 24 years old; infirm since birth and walks with diffi-

15

culty with two crutches. A couple who adopted him at the age of three has five other children. He remembers his happiness when he finally realized that he had some parents who loved him. He always remains thankful for them. Paul is very humble, but his very infirmities could push him toward seeking compensating experiences. His sincerity, honesty, and modesty are evident. The special grace he received in Santa Maria is a benefit for his own life and for its balance but it is not evident that he has a charism or a special mission.

BARBARA MATTHIAS

Barbara Matthias, born January 20, 1947, has been the target so much suffering and opposition that my study of her case expanded disproportionately and this is why I had to make her the topic of another part of this book. I interviewed her privately at Monsignor Rohde's request.

A native of Brazil, she has a humble and pious nature. She was baptized soon after her sixth birthday. Barbara is handicapped by Turner's Syndrome 45 X karyotype: XO instead of XX for the female and XY for the male. As a consequence, she has a short stature (4 feet 8 inches). She is unable to bear children but developed all of the secondary female characteristics through hormone therapy. She had two unfortunate marriages (1967-1977 and 1980-1982). Then Barbara made two attempts at the religious life: first in a convent of cloistered Dominicans (1983-1989) and then in a more active congregation (1989-1990).

On March 24, 1990, she made a pilgrimage to Santa Maria. It was there (at the hill) that she had the apparitions. Charlie Nole, coordinator of the movement, took her into his house for discernment but some conflicts occurred. Charlie wanted to collect pledges of money for the Cross project and according to Barbara, the Virgin said: *"Don't raise money. It will come in its own time."*

Around May 18, 1990, Charlie sent Barbara away from his home attempting to separate her from the group. What followed were all sorts of tribulations. Barbara became caught between assistance from her supporters and the severe trials by her persecutors. The persecutors spoke of having discerned: faking, hallucinating or some infernal action of the devil. She had become a sign of contradiction. However, she astonishingly escaped these opposing traps. Progressively she recuperated and found work at Mc Donald's fast food that allowed her to earn a modest income.

1. Barbara is sincere. Her ecstasy, studied by the Faculty of Medicine in San Francisco, is coherent and not pathological. It is not a result of her handicap. On the contrary, the daily apparitions have allowed her to recuperate balance and a remarkable autonomy. This success and strength calls for esteem and even admiration.

2. Barbara is modest, humble and limpid. Her childhood in Brazil developed some remarkable convincing qualities in her. She radiates a deep and transparent joy which is astonishing in view of her poverty and her problems. It is a joy springing from the depths of her soul.

3. In various circumstances where I observed her (in 1991 and 1992), she was constantly discrete, effaced, and able to facilitate a deep peace that goes beyond the antagonisms raised around her.

4. Her influence has produced good fruits: conversions and healings, under the benefit of verification.

In short, Barbara illustrates the words of the Gospel: *"Blessed Are the Poor."* She assumes patiently, courageously and peacefully the limitations and handicaps of her difficult life without complexity or any ostentation. This renunciation of self is remarkable.

But she is the second seer and may be called to keep a modest role in the groove of the fundamental messages received by Carol Nole who remains the source and foundation of the Cross of Peace movement.

4. An Action of Pastoral Advice

The Leaders

Charlie Nole and his wife Carol took charge of establishing the non profit Cross of Peace Corporation (with salaries that are currently being discussed). They organize and lead the group. The union is deep and the prayer is fervent, persistent and homogeneous, despite a big heterogeneous composition of the group. Americans, Hispanics, and Asians: rich and poor, educated and simple, sick and healthy, young and old, priests and laity, meeting as equals before the Lord.

The Spiritual Responsibility

Monsignor John Rohde, was approved by the Cardinal Archbishop of Los Angeles, Roger M. Mahony and the auxiliary bishop (of the Santa Barbara Pastoral Region), G. Patrick Ziemann, to spiritually guide and pastor this group. He is a gracious man endowed and gifted with numerous talents. As a young priest he was a well known singer and featured star of parish functions. Despite his theological education, his faith is not isolated. He is one of his people. I admire this oneness of spirit that I see in a number of pastors in Italy and America. Some have different styles but they are the essential factor of unity in their Churches which is in contrast to those who disassociate themselves by entering into a critical intellectualism or ideology of the clergy that often bewilders the faithful.

He has carries out his task with great balance, openness, tact and intelligence.

He works judiciously to re-establish peace within the limits of his availability, as he is the pastor of a large parish in Santa Barbara (65 miles south of Santa Maria). His capabilities also made him worthy of an appointment to Episcopal Vicar of the Santa Barbara Pastoral Region, after Bishop Ziemann became the Bishop of the Santa Rosa Diocese.

Sometimes he came on weekends to lead the Cross of Peace prayer meeting or give counsel in cases of difficulty. As a good gardener for God he prevents errors and cultivates the fruit. He was dismissed from this responsibility by the Cross of Peace Corporation on September 10, 1991. But, since taking over his new position as an Episcopal Vicar in the diocese, he has reassumed responsibility on a higher level.

Divisions Overcome

On my first visit to Santa Maria I was surprised by the contrast between the edifying unity and fervor of the group as a whole and the dissensions about Barbara among the more educated people of the group: supporters and detractors equally ardent and active from San Francisco to Los Angeles.

- The construction of the Cross won't happen until a full reconciliation takes place, I told them.

This difficult reconciliation, was facilitated by Monsignor Rohde. He finally convened two successive meetings for peace that everyone prepared for in prayer:

-A large assembly of people August 22, 1992

-Then a restricted meeting of community leaders on September 1, 1992, where I was present in Santa Maria at the home of Bob and Jerrie Castro.

As a result of these meetings, Charlie Nole, a strong man whom some would reproach as having a domineering personality, astonished everyone by writing to Monsignor Rohde this profoundly humble and conciliatory letter in which he notably says:

Please accept my apology for any part of the misunderstanding and confusion that might have arisen due to our mishandling of the situation with Barbara. As you stated, the business of apparitions, how to work with and interpret messages, was something very new to all of us. After viewing the testing and indepth work done to verify the apparition, I will henceforth leave the responsibility of verification to the experts. Our complete focus will be on the mission of building the Cross of Peace as asked for by Mary in her messages to Carol.

Building a Community
of Faith and Prayer

What is remarkable in the history of this group, despite obstacles that prevent building the Cross, is that the group is judiciously reconverting itself with an effort to sustaining fruitful prayer and spiritual formation.

While celebrating with them on July 27-28, 1991, I felt a lovely quality of receptivity and prayer founded on a simple love of Christ and the Virgin Mary. These people who for the most part come from modest means, various social levels and ethnic backgrounds (Anglos, Mexicans, Asians), pray and communicate in perfect harmony.

I had the feeling there of recovering what the Bible calls *"The Poor of Yahweh."* These humble people, strangers to ideological speculations, seek God without deviation finding Him in the fullness of their life: personal, domestic and social. In an hour where mainstream Christianity has become the prey of ideologies of the sects the stimulus of apparitions and charisms appear as a providential antidote. One sees in Santa Maria the flowering of spiritual sensitivity, generosity, the giving of self and holiness of the humble which are the very foundations of the Church.

Apparitions, visions, and locutions call for discernment but not a systematic refusal and repression. The scandal is not that they occur, rather, it would be whether the Church of today has contradicted the statute of faith in the charisms prophesied by Joel (3:1-5 NJB) and proclaimed by the Apostle Peter on the day of Pentecost: **"In the last days- the Lord declares- I shall pour out my Spirit on all humanity, Your sons and daughters shall prophesy, your young people shall see visions, your old people dream dreams."** (Acts 2:17-21 NJB). When this happens must we to be astonished? Are we to be grieved? Is it necessary to repress? It would be better to welcome, discerne and channel these normal phenomen under the benefit of discernment. They are not necessarily extraordinary or miraculous but are the humble means that God puts at the disposal man for guiding him through the visible to the invisible: by visible signs of the invisible God.

The projects of Santa Maria are in suspension but life progresses and the assurance is great, despite so many hurdles:

"The Virgin has told us everything will be accomplished," someone repeated to me.

Meanwhile, one obeys and one prays. May the future confirm this trust, docility and patient prayer. Wherever the Holy Spirit is at work temptations emerge and divisions can be frequent as in Corinth during the time of St Paul (as I mentioned previously).

In Santa Maria the temptations were strong but the Christians are reacting well. The discrete action of the responsible ecclesiastical authority and priests who have led weekends of prayer are overcoming divisions and tensions. The poisonous fruits of Satan have declined. The fruits of the Holy Spirit do not cease to prosper.

Appendix

The Consequences of Adversaries

The group who welcomed me to Santa Maria Saturday July 27, 1991 was meeting, until my arrival, in a good location at St. Joseph's Church in Nipomo, Ca. for 16 hours of prayer every weekend. This is where their weekend with me was supposed to take place. But, 15 days before, the pastor who had recently returned from Ireland threw the group out of the parish hall. Someone had told him negative things about Medjugorje. When this group who was favorable to Medjugorje wanted him to meet Fr. Laurentin, author, of several books on these "forsaken apparitions," it caused the pastor to break his realitiionship with the group.

I attempted to go and see him according to the principles of the Gospel: "If your brother has something against you, go first and reconcile with your brother." More often than not, with God's help, Christians succeed in reconciling even though one pays the price in the form of humiliation.

The robust pastor appeared at the door with a stern face. To my amiable words of greeting his opposition was evident:

"The bishops of Ireland condemned Medjugorje. I just returned from there and I know!".

He used the excuse that the Irish bishop's had taken a position like some of the bishops in Yugoslavia which has been distorted by tenacious advesarious. I tried to enlighten him.

Do you know that more than a 100 bishops from around world went on pilgrimage to Medjugorje, last year? A number of them went on this pilgrimage only after having consulted the Pope, who encouraged them to go.

But not the Irish bishops!, he protested. Mr. Michael Jones enlightened me.

Mr. Jones is a man who practices my same (Catholic) faith, but he is a polemist who relishes scandal.

Then I showed him my books so that I could help him understand the seriousness of my research. I informed him that the Pope read my first two books and had thanked me for them. He didn't listen:

"You are controversial, he interrupted, and you just write for the business.

Nevertheless, I looked for a common point of understanding:

We are both priests, in the service of Lord, you as the pastor of a good parish. I also try like you to serve Him well. Wouldn't it be best if we could take the step to offer each other peace?

My mind is made up.

The tone of his voice indicated we could not communicate any further. It was useless to insist. I attempted to conclude on a ground of peace that would unite us beyond our dispute:

I will pray for you and your good parish.

Pray for me? You want humiliate me! Am I a sinner?

We are all sinners, I in any case. I ask for your prayers and also for your blessing.

To repair the humiliation of which he complained, I knelt to receive his blessing with the hope that this call to a ministerial gesture would re-establish a fraternal tie between us. This was the final chance of reconciliation. But the blessing fell hard, like a cold tomb of contempt. When I stood up, he did not extend his hand. I understood that if I offered my hand to him, he wouldn't accept it. At best it was worth it to avoid the worst. I thanked him for his blessing, but he turned briskly toward the church hall where he had left a parish breakfast.

For my visit, the prayer group that had been evicted from this parish, rented the gymnasium. They won't be able to do this every weekend as it would be too expensive.

We have found a site in the park for our meetings, they said.

What will you do when it is winter or when it's raining?

We will bring some umbrellas.

I was happy to share in their prayer and their poverty. They know how to rejoice in serving the Lord, even in adversity.

Finis

PART II

Beyond the Wisdom of the Wise

An article I had written on the apparations and the Cross of Peace in Santa Maria should have appeared in May, 1992 in *Stella Maris*. One of the secondary visionaries, Barbara Matthias, was ardently contested by some and supported by others. From two sides I received dozens of faxes for and against her. The supporters did not spare themselves. They spent twenty thousand dollars to submit Barbara to scientific tests of a very high level. This was risky because these tests, objectively done by non Catholic doctors, could have been negative. As for the opponents, they multiplied their investigations of Barbara's matrimonial and religious failures. Thus, they methodically played the role of devil's advocate: a useful function since it is anticipated in the process of canonization.

1. I saw friendships becoming obscured by the fact that I did not agree with the conclusions of the opponents. For these reasons, I decided to withdraw my article scheduled for publication in May of 1992. Stella Maris regretted this decision.

2. Concerned with peace and objectivity I pursued my discernment. I followed one contact after another, with the sole thought of approaching the truth as closely as possible. This is the result:

I received hundreds of pieces of information for review. In spite of my concern for brevity, the length of the article resulted in an inconvenient expansion of the importance of Barbara, counter to the conclusion that had placed her calling into discretion. Should it be published? I did not know. I sent the manuscript to the interested parties almost like a bottle thrown into the sea.

1. The History of Barbara Matthias

Barbara Matthias is almost an unknown person. She was born January 20, 1947, at 12:40 P. M. in Rio de Janeiro, Brazil of Maximillian Paul Matthias (1898-1953), a regional manager of Pepsi Cola and Marie Adelaid Ferreira (October 17, 1910- May 9, 1981). She has two brothers with the same mother: Patrick Allen born October 16, 1935, of a first marriage to Edward Clark, (who died shortly afterward); and Paul Brian, born the May 7, 1943, of the second marriage with M.P. Matthias.

Barbara kept a sense of jovialness from her Brazilian childhood that was not altered by immigrating to the United States. She was five years old when her family transferred to New Jersey (USA). From the age of three or four she had a profound sense of being created by God. At the age of five she asked to be baptized. Her mother (Catholic) told her that her father (Anglican) wanted her to wait until she was older: then she could make a more informed choice. But Barbara had heard the stories of Jesus and the saints read to her and she had the desire to become a saint herself. She had always been fervent.

At the age of six in New Jersey, she recounted that when she was in bed, she heard an inner voice (audible voice within) gently warning her that her father (55 years old) would die the next day: "...*but, you should not warn your mother and your brothers,*" said the voice, whom Barbara considered to be "the voice of God." The next day her father died of a heart attack in a neighbor's house. Barbara did not learn of it immediately. On this autumn day of 1953, her brother Brian entered the house after baseball practice, asking: ***"Why is there an ambulance in front of the neighbor's door?"*** Barbara answered him, "*it's Dad! Dad will die!*" Brian did not believe her and ran to the neighbor's door. It was so.

Shortly after her father's death Barbara asked again to be baptized. This time her mother accepted, both for Barbara and for her brother Brian: in the Catholic Church. Barbara remembers that her life with God became fortified. As soon as she could make her first Communion, she received the Eucharist frequently.

Barbara was an applied student but she preferred religion to mathematics. From 1954 she received her education at Catholic schools in Colton, and San Bernardino, California. However, the last three years were obtained at the Colton public high school because her mother lacked money for private education.

During her adolescence her companions tried to encourage her to conform to their way of teen style: hair fashion, dress and makeup. She replaced her glasses (worn since age eleven) with contact lenses that she wore for several years without adapting to them. She resumed wearing her glasses after her high school graduation. Her small stature was the reason she was chosen to be the school "mascot". However, this role did not please her.

At the age of sixteen her slow development required medical consultations. The doctors diagnosed Turner's Syndrome, (45 X karyotype: XO instead of XX for the woman and XY for the man: (a typical karyotype, Dr. Conte, of UC San Francisco, a specialist in this syndrome, specified.) This genetic abnormality (gonadic dysgenesis) limited her development: short stature (Barbara measured 1 m 43:4 ft 8.5 inches) and ovarian insufficiency, resulting in sterility. She has developed all the secondary female characteristics through hormone therapy.

An Unfortunate Marriage

After completing her secondary studies (high school graduation in 1965), Barbara married A. S. July 15, 1967, without hope of bearing children. Her husband became a violent, abusive alcoholic subjecting her to severe trials. She surmounted her suffering by prayer and attendance at daily Mass. She also became a Third Order Franciscan. They had taken a foster child through Social Services but had to return him because of the deteriorating home life.

Two Apparitions

In 1974, Barbara had a second profound religious experience while walking with her friend Cindy on the grounds at Mission San Luis Rey. She again heard the audible voice within that she had perceived at the age of six.

The voice guided me toward the rose gar den (where a statue of the Virgin stood).
I heard distinctly:
*Take the hands of the blessed Mother, **the voice said.***

When she took the hands of the statue it became animated in a brilliant aura of light. Barbara was overwhelmed to see the hands of stone become hands of flesh. Then the Virgin spoke to her:

My Son and I love you and we want to let you know how much we love you.
I love you both with all my heart, answered Barbara.
We know that you love us. That is why we called you here.
What do you want to tell me?
My Son has a message for you.
What is the message?
It is not I who will give it to you.
First go to the left and touch one red rose, only one!

Then Barbara was directed by the Virgin to stand under a large tree, near a white wall in the southwest section of the garden, and wait in prayer. It was then that she saw the holy face of Jesus on the garden wall. His head was crowned with thorns and He was crying. His face was two dimensional and surrounded by a bright light.

Why are you crying? Barbara asked.
Because I am here with all of my love and so
many people do not love me in return. I wish
people would give me just a little love.
People have time for everything except Me.
Tell people I am waiting for them and how
much.
How can I do this? questioned Barbara.
I will give you the courage to do as I ask.

Then Jesus announced His departure.

May I go with you? asked Barbara..

You may not do so now. You have My work
to do. I know how
much you love Me, and I promise that I will
return to you in two years.

Then the apparition disappeared. Barbara con-
fided her conversation with apparition to her
friend Cindy, who seemed to be afraid:

What's wrong? inquired Barbara.
Your face and your hair are glowing like a
neon light!
she replied.

Barbara convinced her not to be afraid and they
returned to the statue of Mary that was still
animated. Barbara said to the Virgin:

*I have received the message and I will do what Jesus has asked
me to do.*

Mary nodded with an approving smile and said to Barbara:

*As testimony to your obedience, go and see he rose that
you touched.*

She looked at the rose again. It was glowing brilliantly with a white light. The other roses had kept their natural red color. On returning to the statue, the Virgin had disappeared.

Barbara persevered and two years later (in 1976) the promise of Jesus became a realization.

It was during my retreat at Vista, California. My friend and I were waiting in front of St. Francis of Assisi Church for a ride home when I was inspired by the words of Jesus in the Gospel: 'Knock and the door shall be opened to you.'

Barbara and her friend headed for the church door and found it closed. Then they smelled a strong odor of roses, yet there were no roses around the church. They went around to the side of the building to see if there was another door open. All of the doors were closed, but a window was open and they looked through the window: They saw Jesus walking back and forth in front of the altar, as if in meditation. He looked to be about 30 years old and was dressed in a white robe.

Is it you Jesus? Asked Barbara.

He nodded His head and said:

Did I not tell you that I would see you again in two years? I always keep my promises. I am happy that you have followed the mes ages. Continue to spread them, and now I must leave.
May I go with you? I love you very much, asked Barbara.
You may not come with me now, because you must do what I have asked, but I will be with you and you will feel my presence. When you die, I promise I will come to take you home with me.

Then He disappeared.

Did you hear what Jesus said? Barbara

asked her friend.
I only saw Jesus but could not hear what He
was saying to you,
she replied.

(Testimony of Barbara given to Jerrie Castro
9-30-91)

Second Unhappy Marriage

Shortly afterward, her alcoholic husband, who was following a course of therapy, fell in love with a married woman who was in his therapy group. He filed for a civil divorce May 25, 1977. The final civil dissolution was granted December 16, 1977. Barbara subsequently filed for a Church annulment that was granted May 15, 1980.

On August 18, 1980 (three and one half years after her divorce from A. S.) she married D. S. in a civil ceremony. He was not a Catholic. She hoped that he would become Catholic and that the marriage would eventually be validated in the Church. But this new husband was not much better than the first. He left her in 1981. Barbara filed for a divorce October 21, 1982 and it became final May 11, 1983.

After her separation from D. S., Barbara moved in with a friend and also cared for her mother (at her home) who had severe rheumatoid arthritis. She helped in the CCD program at her parish and continued her college studies. In May of 1983 she received a Bachelor of Arts Degree from California State University, San Bernardino.

Two Attempts of the Religious Life: 1983-1990

Barbara then made two attempts at the religious life. The first one at Perpetual Rosary Monastery, a cloistered Dominican convent located in Syracuse, New York. Barbara arrived there August 13, 1983. She became a postulant October 7th. But in May, 1989, three months before her solemn profession of final vows, the superiors gave a negative judgment for her contemplative vocation. They appreciated her great piety and were assured of her scruples, but a certain lack of good sense and adaptation to the very demanding community life was problem for her.

A religious psychologist was consulted. She discouraged her from remaining in the cloister but did not object to her religious vocation. She advised Barbara to continue but in an active community. Following this advice, she entered (as an inquirer) the Dominican Sisters of Hawthorne who care for cancer patients (October 1989 to January, 1990). However, the task proved to be too rough on her health and temperament. She was judged to be insufficiently flexible for the religious life. She moved back to California after leaving the convent.

Briefly, this was a failure on all fronts: her two marriages without hope of children as well as her two attempts at the religious life. Barbara was then 43 years old.

First Apparitions at Santa Maria (March 24-May 11, 1990)

Barbara made a pilgrimage to Santa Maria. On March 24, 1990 she had her first apparition at the site of the future Cross of Peace and submitted her message to Charlie Nole, coordinator of the movement. She returned the following Wednesday, March 28, and received another message. Charlie informed Monsignor John Rohde, Spiritual Director of the project and requested her to return the following weekend. Charlie then insisted that Barbara abandon her work in Woodland Hills and come to live with him and his wife in Santa Maria: the

45

transfer took place March 31. Since that time, she has had daily apparitions. Charlie required that she write everything down as soon as possible (everything that happened to her) which often caused her to sit up late into the night. Barbara appreciated the gentleness of Carol (the locutionist and wife of Charlie) but felt submissively crushed by the powerful and unreasonable personality of her husband. On his insistent demands she noted too meticulously and too laboriously, the messages from the Virgin, thus mixing in her own interpretations and commentaries. Her awkward wording invited the side of criticism.

Eventually, the messages created a conflict: On May 8th Charlie launched a fund raising campaign for the Cross of Peace project: operations, administration and living expenses for himself, Carol and Barbara. According to Barbara, the Virgin was not pleased with this idea. *"The money would come freely in time,"* the Virgin said. The regional bishop (G. Patrick Ziemann) also intervened and demanded that all fund raising terminate; any money collected from pledges would have to be returned.

Tribulations (May 18, 1990-February 28, 1992)

In mid May 1990, Charlie concluded there was no authenticity. He decided to send Barbara away.

On May 18th or 19th, during the apparition, Barbara received this personal message:

During this present persecution all seems mortal and somber...the storm is raging presently. After all storms there is a rainbow. The rainbow is ahead of you. I assure you that the storm will pass, and you will see that it was worthwhile to go through it to see the rainbow.

(The Message is dated May 18th around noon, but seems to be the next day as there was disorder in the transcription during these perturbed times).

Several days prior, two young women, collected Barbara's belongings (which had been packed at the Noles) and moved her in to their apartment. Charlie wanted Barbara to be as far away from Santa Maria as possible because she now seemed to constitute an annoying interference for him. So, he arranged for the two young women to take Barbara to Woodland Hills (her previous home with her niece- near Los Angeles) on May 19, 1990 for a meeting with her brother and family.

Before leaving Santa Maria, the two women took her to the site of the future Cross for a "final" visit. Charlie even came to encourage her. The Virgin confirmed to Barbara that she would now pass through a great persecution. Soon afterward, the two women who had packed all of her possessions into the trunk of their car (unknown to Barbara) proceeded to drive her, in spite of her protests, to Woodland Hills.

"I want to get out and return to Santa Maria," she begged.

The two women dramatically stated that Charlie had told them she was suicidal. Barbara wanted to get out of the car but the speed was too great. They told her they had orders to take her to her brother and they were not going to allow her to stay in Santa Maria.

There were heavy words at her brother's where another apparition comforted her during the evening. Everyone wanted to have her examined at a mental health clinic. The police were contacted with the idea of having them commit her. But, the officers were not convinced.

"Why should we commit her? It is not our job." "But she claims to see the Virgin Mary!", they said. *"That's not a crime, and, so what if she does see her?"*, the officers answered humorously.

After midnight, at the end of a long discussion, with the group Barbara agreed to go to the clinic:

"We will therefore have proof that the Virgin does not want me to be committed to a psychiatric hospital!", she said.

After many hours of examination, the doctor concluded there was no reason to keep her.

On Sunday May 20, the two women came to get the latest news and were surprised to find Barbara at her niece's house with her brother.

"Will you take me back to Santa Maria?," Barbara asked.

Despite one hour of deliberation, they unloaded her things and left alone to go back to Santa Maria.

During this long day Barbara was able to explain everything to her family. Enlightenment ended with a reconciliation and her brother returned her to Santa Maria, Monday May 21, 1990 without believing in the apparitions, Barbara stated.

He left her in a motel for the first night. The next night she found refuge at the Good Samaritan Shelter for the homeless, as she didn't have much money. A girl named Cathy took her into her home for several days where Barbara took care of the house while she was away. After that, a woman named Joni Kovarik took her in until approximately June 23. And then, again, she was outside on the streets. She found asylum (through Joni Kovarik) in a disreputable hotel, inhabited by cockroaches and bugs; prostitutes; drug users and alcoholics- an underworld not recommended! One day a woman was found there who had been suffocated under her pillow.

Reconquest of Independence

Barbara's handicap and her serere hearing loss (a consequence of Turner's Syndrome) hindered her search for work: her lack of organizational skills kept her from obtaining a job with good wages, certainly due to her because she was handicapped. She did find part time employment with McDonald's Fast Food but this was not sufficient to pay the hotel and allowed her almost nothing to eat. In addition, McDonald's progressively reduced her work hours from five hours per day to two hours per week with a salary reduction accordingly, veering toward total elimination. She was nothing but a stopgap. Luckily for her, these arbitrary restrictions were denounced by the Department of Employment as "discrimination against the handicapped." Barbara recuperated 25 hrs of work per week, which then assured her a strict minimum of vital resources. But her health had suffered from these conditions of a life of disaster. She lost 20 pounds. She had weighed 100 pounds.

John and Barbara Gayton rescued her from this sad state and gave her boarding from July, 1991 to February, 1992. Their kind hospitality soon caused her to be criticized by others as a parasite.

In March 1992, two years after her first apparitions, she recovered her autonomy: at present she lives in a modest apartment with her friend Eleanor Esquevil, a young looking retired lady. Barbara pays her share of the rent and provides her own food, different from that of her companion, following the habits of her Brazilian childhood.

The apartment is located directly in front of the Catholic church. This is where I visited her on September 1, 1992. The neighborhood is modest and nicely built in a Spanish style. She lives on the second floor which has access by an exterior staircase (as in Quebec City). The apartment is furnished with thick wall to wall carpeting. Barbara occupies one bedroom, small, but in good order with religious statues and pictures. This is where she has her apparition lasting for two hours, more or less, starting between 4:20 and 4:40 P. M.

Evolution of Apparitions

Barbara's apparitions, which were public at the time she resided in the home of Charlie Nole (March to May, 1990), became progressively longer.

30 minutes, March 24
45 minutes, March 28
50 minutes, March 31
65 minutes, April 2
75 minutes, April 4
90 minutes, April 11
140 minutes, April 22
155 minutes, April 23
235 minutes, April 27
290 minutes, April 29
255 minutes, May 1

265 minutes, May 3
325 minutes, May 8
385 minutes, May 10
413 minutes, May 11
290 minutes, May 16
390 minutes, May 17 and 18

Afterwards, the length of the apparitions returned to an average of three hours and thirty minutes: The last one which was timed on Wednesday, July 4, 1990, (the ninety first), lasted for 360 minutes.

After May 21, 1990 the apparitions had taken on a private character. Barbara liked to be at St. Mary of the Assumption Church, (where since the beginning of March, 1992 her residence has been directly across the street). By October 1990 the time of the apparition had decreased to three hours and the length of the message averaged three pages. In December 1990 the time of the apparition decreased to one and one half to two hours.

In the summer of 1992 the pastor of the parish forbid her from coming to the church to receive the apparition. One afternoon (according to the testimony of a woman who was seated in the front pew), he entered the church in a state of anger; tried to pick Barbara up (just as she was coming out of the ecstasy) and remove her from the building. A heated discussion took place between the pastor and the woman who had observed his actions. Barbara was frightened by the incident and promised the pastor she would obey. Since that time she receives them at home.

A team of lay ministers assist her in Santa Maria along with her spiritual director, Father David Link of Concord, California who guides her in discerning the apparition and the formulation of the messages. The apparitions still occur daily. They still start between 4:20 and 4:40 in the afternoon and last from one hour and 15 minutes to two hours depending on the Virgin.

2. OBJECTIONS

Barbara has been discussed very much. Many factors played against her:

-Her genetic chromosome handicap limited her adaptation to a routine life.

-Her hearing impairment limited her range of possibilities for employment.

54

This last problem was finally overcome in 1991 with binaural hearing aids, provided by Anna Marie Maagdenberg, a specialist in audiology. We also have seen how Barbara has attained an independent lifestyle since March, 1992.

During the exuberant period of her first ecstasies, many points astounded and shocked her adversaries:

1. Sunday April 1, 1990, Our Lady said:

I wish to have the title, Our Lady of the Immaculate Heart. This title pleases me very much.

"To put Our Lady in front of 'The Immaculate Heart' is a useless complication," one objects.

My answer is: This title is not new. It dates back to Catherine Laboure, many of the classic devotions have more complicated titles and the reference to the Immaculate Heart is above criticism.

2. On April 16, 1990 she received this message:

My child, see the doorway to Heaven. (at that time Mary showed Barbara a door to Heaven.) The Secret to opening this door is to love me, remain faithful and avoid the things of this world which are hindrances to Eternal life in heaven.

"Is it normal that Mary would even place herself before God?" observed one.

My answer is: The messages of Medjugorje and elsewhere pose analogous problems.

3. On April 21, 1990 she received this message:

Today, I have revealed to you one of the deepest secrets I have in my heart. It con cerns the end of the world. Barbara will carry this secret in her heart and it will be very difficult for her to bear.

The adversaries object:

"'As to the exact day or the hour, no one knows it, neither the angels in Heaven nor even the Son, but only the Father.'(Mk: 13, 32) Jesus himself said this" they quoted.

My answer is: The message did not reveal to Barbara either the day or the hour.

4. On April 27, during the course of an apparition lasting 235 minutes, the Virgin said:

Each time that you prayed the Rosary, I prayed with you. Mary had a large Rosary and used it.

"The Virgin cannot pray to herself", one objected.

My answer is: In fact, as it was in Lourdes, the Virgin has a "Rosary in hand," but only moves her lips for the Our Father and the Gloria. Barbara precisely stated to me that it was the same with her.

5. May 10, 1990, Juan Diego (the seer of Guadalupe: 1531), appeared with the Virgin and offered his Mexican hat to her. T h e Virgin donned it and danced. Does the local color and "humor" suffice to justify this peculiarity? (pages 133 and 144 of the typewritten compilation of messages).

I submitted this objection to Barbara. She told me in substance:

One must understand the circumstances. May 5th had been a Mexican feast day (Cinco de Mayo). Many joyful Hispanics were present during the apparitions with musical instruments. This was also during time the Pope had journeyed to Mexico where he had beatified Juan Diego. It was under these circumstances that he appeared to me with the Virgin. He bowed his head in front of her. She was touched by his humility and simplicity of heart. She asked him for his hat and he placed it on her head. For a moment she began a dance step as if to associate with the joy of the Hispanic people who came to the apparitions.

6. "Since Barbara was sterile, did she have the right to marry?" My answer is: Yes, sterility is not a canonical impediment.

7. The adversaries claimed she had not obtained a Church annulment of her first marriage until her second husband had left her. I have reviewed the official civil and Church documents of her marriages and divorces. Barbara did not marry her second husband D. S. until after she had obtained a Church annulment of the first marriage to A. S. Therefore, the claim of the adversaries is not valid.

Barbara loyally recognized that it was an error and a mistake to marry her second husband outside the church (civil marriage only-1980). She repented and confessed, and for along time was weighted down by scruples after this digression. Her supporters emphasized in her favor that the civil marriage of Charlie and Carol Nole (the locutionist) preceded the annulment of Charlie's former marriage. His annulment was not obtained until autumn of 1988 because the dossier had to be transferred from an Oklahoma diocesan marriage tribunal to the Los Angeles Archdiocesan marriage tribunal. The Nole's marriage was validated in the Church in late 1988.

None of these objections disqualify Barbara. Some are explained by the groping difficulties in surmounting her handicaps: others, by the awkwardness of wording in her messages which attributed to malicious interpretations. But a number of apparitions, including the recognized ones, also present disconcerting peculiarities. If these objections harm credibility, and if they call for caution, they are generally explainable accidents of circumstance, well overcome.

As for disqualifying Barbara because of Turner's Syndrome, this falls into a racism of the anti-handicapped in the name of eugenics (the science of bringing about an improved type of offspring of the human species), which in our century praises the abortion of all infants who might present any probability of anomaly, large or small. The handicapped form a segment of the poor, who are privileged by Christ. Furthermore, the achievements of Barbara, who recovered a normal life of independence, do not merit contempt but esteem and even admiration.

8. An objection apparently more serious and more radical: Barbara's first spiritual director, Msgr. John Rohde, took a position against her in 1990, on two accounts:

A. In a letter dated May 29, 1990, he accused Barbara of being disobedient to him. But he later understood that Barbara's apparent disobedience resulted from a misunderstanding, due to a communication error. She did not believe that a request transmitted through Charlie had come from the Monsignor. This objection has been totally resolved.

B. More seriously, July 6, 1990, he writes to her:

"The alleged apparitions and messages are not of the Virgin Mary. I am saying this after a long and hard study. You are convinced that it is real and I am not...I do not accept these apparitions and messages as authentic. I cannot let non authenticity harm the people of God. I have this responsibility as spiritual director." (Letter of July 6, 1990).

When I met Msgr. Rohde in Santa Maria, at the end of July, 1991, he did not mention this negative judgment already passed. On the contrary, he wanted me to meet Barbara discretely, without attempting to influence my opinion or discernment. He desired for me to become quietly enlightened.

I then met Barbara privately with a sympathetic group of her friends and supporters at the home of Bob and Jerrie Castro. I was impressed by her joyful, childlike simplicity. Her weakness and small stature, contrasted with her formidable energy; her frailty with a great intensity for life and a great confidence in the apparitions, as well as a grand ease and liveliness in her movements.

3. THE TESTS IN SAN FRANCISCO, SEPTEMBER-OCTOBER 1991

In the autumn of 1991, with the consent of the Holy Virgin and Barbara who was perfectly docile and cooperative, a group of medical doctors of very high caliber conducted a multi-disciplined series of tests on her at the University of California, San Francisco Medical Center.

Monsignor Rohde then reached this conclusion:

"There is no faking or pretending. These ecstasies do not have a psychotic or organic etiology. I am satisfied with the sincerity of Barbara Matthias." (Letter dated and signed by Msgr. Rohde and transmitted to me by FAX, February 10, 1992).

Subsequently for him, the question is open. The ecstasies are not medically pathological. He encouraged medical studies. He participated in them and understood the tests of touching the apparition guided by Barbara's hand. Certain individuals among those who performed this test felt nothing. Others felt a pressure, never the sensation of a true resis-

tance nor the grip of a hand. This vague sensation does not constitute a proof. If a doctor,
who is a specialist in touch had made this
affidavit, he would not necessarily be exempt
from the snare of subjectivity; other doctors
who had performed the same tests in front of
me elsewhere had clearly concluded: the im-
pressions which we were able to obtain, in all
spiritual openness to the phenomena, do not
have any character of an objective palpation or
sensation. One can draw no conclusion, neither
medical nor scientific.

Barbara's psychological tests brought to
light small deficiencies pertaining to Turner's
Syndrome: difficulty in orientation, weakness
on structural tasks but without disorder the
report stated.

The psychological tests:
<u>Minnesota Multiphasic Personality Inventory</u>
<u>(MMPI)</u>
<u>Millon Clinical Multiaxil Clinical Inventory 2</u>
<u>(MCMII)</u>
<u>Thematic Apperception Test (TAT)</u>
<u>Rorschach</u>

These tests showed a high degree of selec-
tivity in the experiences reported. Barbara did
not present disordered feelings or thoughts:

there is no personality disorder; her religious experience favors a coherent equilibrium.

The psychological tests which evaluated her ability to interpret facial expressions were normal; weak only in evaluating the <u>intensity</u> of emotions that were portrayed on the faces.

The cerebral Magnetic Resonance Imaging (MRI), a more sensitive technique than the scanner, showed a minor atrophy of the vertex (superior part of the cortex) but without structural pathology. It is essentially normal.

The nine neuropsychological tests, conducted in San Francisco, revealed the difficulties Barbara has in the visual and spacial domain, but without structural disorder.

The ecstasies do not reflect a post traumatic stress disorder from the rough years with her alcoholic ex-husband.

The psychiatric evaluation did not show evidence of a personality disorder or schizophrenia.

Briefly, Barbara has surmounted her handicap very well by a good utilization of her reduced means. The apparitions have helped her to find her equilibrium.

The Ecstasy

During the ecstasy (which is preceded by a phase of pre-ecstasy), Barbara has her eyes open. Ocular movements, as well as all blinking of the eyes, cease at the beginning of the ecstasy and her voice disappears when she speaks to the apparition; there is movement of the lips without speech: all traits which are also established at Medjugorje.

There is no facial expression, except rarely when her face reflects the joy or sadness of the apparition (as at Lourdes).

Pulse and respirations are extremely regular but slowed down. There is dilation of the peripheral vessels. The activity of the sweat glands is reduced but not stopped.

The ecstasy manifests a state of relaxation and meditation. There is concentration and immobility without catalepsy.

During the ecstasy the electro-encephalogram records a diminishing of the beta waves (reflection) and an augmentation of the alpha waves (contemplation), which characterizes a profound state of meditation without anything abnormal or pathological.

Barbara is disconnected from the environment. She is insensitive to embarrassing or painful tests. The injection of ice water into the ears (done in the laboratory of Anna Marie Maagdenberg, M.S., N. P.), provoked no reaction: except a negligible contraction of the chin observable in normal life. In the same way swallowing was rare, as the profound disconnection causes infrequent swallowing.

Moreover, according to a test reviewed three times by different American doctors and technicians in October, 1991, she had no photomotor reflexes to the projection of a sharp light on the eyes. This reflex did not pass through the brain but only through the cerebral cortex showing that the disconnection went as far as this level. But in September 1992, this same test conducted by Philippe Loron M. D. and Antoine Mansour M. D. caused a reaction. The ecstasy is not necessarily constant.

Barbara's disconnection is perhaps as it seems, partial and superficial, because she guides with control the hand of the individuals she wants to touch the apparition: therefore she perceives them. Without a doubt, the manner is very particular but limited. She does not see or hear them. She does not perceive them in a normal fashion. She explained that <u>it is on the indication of Virgin that she intervenes</u> by taking the hand and guiding it to her. Our observation confirms this explanation.

Barbara emerges from the ecstasy without confusion or disorientation in spite of the depth of the ecstasy:

-This compares her to the seers of Medjugorje who moreover keep their photomoter reflexes.

-It differentiates her from the seers of Kibeho who collapsed peacefully on the ground, at the end of their profound ecstasy and then pass through a time of "resting in the Spirit", for a progressive readaptation to the exterior world. By the end of the ecstasy, Barbara communicates normally in a coherent manner. She then asks for paper to write down the message.

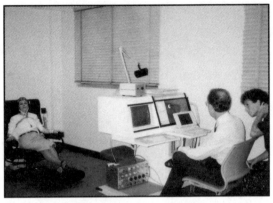

Dr. Charles Yingling conducts EEG study of ecstasy on Barbara Matthias, at UC San Francisco and explains test procedures to Barbara before starting.

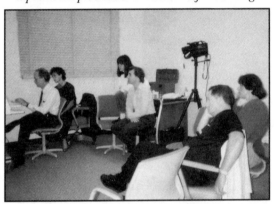

Msgr. John W. Rohde observes testing sessions by investigators.

Fr. Renne Laurentin consults with Dr. Charles Yingling and Dr. Linda Davenport after reviewing results of scientific tests.

3. DISCERNMENT

The spiritual discernment is a result of multiple conclusions which were obtained from Barbara's history, by the scientific tests and by observation.

The Ecstasy

Barbara's ecstasies are spontaneous and not pretended. The clinical tests and observations, achieved with more sophisticated scientific equipment than at Medjugorje or Kibeho, (20 curves for the electroencephalogram) reveal a very profound ecstasy. Even the cerebral cortex is partially disconnected: this is not the case with Medjugorje where the ecstasy is less profound. Barbara's state of ecstasy is coherent and functional. It conditions her contact with the apparition. Her ecstasy is not pathological. She presents rather, a functional nature, according to the measure in which the disconnection with the ambient world conditions a coherent contact with the other world that she witnesses.

The doctors ruled out hysteria, hypnosis, auto-suggestion, epilepsy (by EEG), catalepsy, organic diseases or other pathological causes, as justifications for the ecstasies. Therefore, these ecstasies depend on an unknown and unfounded cause which Barbara witnesses in a coherent manner, as do the other seers.

Barbara's first messages (March to July 1990) do not have the preciseness, the transparency, the gravity, or the simplicity of those of Carol Nole. But, she has overcome her initial failings very well. The wording of her messages, disturbed by the demands of Charlie Nole; by her naivety and her awkwardness, has found its maturity today.

In what measure do these ecstasies explain themselves as natural or supernatural causes? It is always difficult to separate.

1. As with all knowledge it is difficult to discern the subjective and the objective, as the subject and the object are narrowly implied in all knowledge; even in perceptible elementary knowledge. If I see a green tree it is by the subjective impact of this image inverted on the retina of my eye. The stimulus of this image provokes the transmission of an electrical influx (signal) along the optic nerve. The knowledge that results (by deciphering the signals) is that which the subject knows. It is an action of

the subject. This does not prevent knowledge from <u>attaining knowledge of a real and intentional object.</u> The part of the subject and the object is still more difficult to determine in the case of an ecstatic apparition.

2. The primary cause (God) and the secondary cause (the subject) are again, more or less dissociated and difficult to discern, since the first cause penetrates and integrally evokes the second cause. This is why the theologian must necessarily remain prudent in order to evaluate the authenticity of an apparition. The objective that he must not rush to exclude, in any case, is that of a material perception. At Medjugorje or elsewhere, the persons who surround the seers do not perceive the apparition. They have no retinal image. The contact, whether real and objective, is made in another manner. It is an interpersonal and immediate communication which seems to reach the visual and auditory centers of perception.

Barbara's opponents insist that she had a subjective predisposition to being a clairvoyant:

"It was before her baptism that she had a premonition of the death of her father. It is therefore a natural phenomenon rather than a

supernatural one," they say.

To this, one can reply that Barbara already had the Baptism of Desire. She had asked her mother to receive baptism since she was 4 years old and she remembers having being gratified by the sense of the presence of God the Creator. She, therefore, already had a supernatural life.

Her brother stated that she had been pious since childhood. Then she had two isolated apparitions two years apart: 1974 and 1976, shortly before her 30th birthday. The remainder followed. Therefore, Barbara did have a certain receptive disposition. But, it would be difficult to reduce everything to the subjective. Thus, her daily apparitions since March 1990, suggest the hypothesis that the apparitions are spontaneous. The sporadic character and the very time span between the former phenomenon, gives witness to a gratuitous phenomenon (favor or gift from God).

Her sincerity and her coherence testify for the authenticity of Barbara's spiritual communications, taking into consideration the relativities of such a discernment.

In brief, for Barbara as for the other visionaries, the apparitions are not the Beatific Vision but a limited communication, which engages filtered and adapted in various degrees by the receptivity, participation, activity, and interpretation of the subject. Let us emphasize that when Barbara is in ecstasy, she is in a state of real prayer, and at least in this sense it is a true communication.

Spiritual Life

Barbara's spiritual life should be placed in the framework of her ordinary life. What immediately strikes the observer from the exterior are the traits of Barbara's handicap (Turner's Syndrome) which could cause doubt. Does this handicap disqualify her credibility? It is relative in one sense. The juvenile side of her development weakens her authority. But, Jesus said:

"In truth I tell you, unless you change and become like little children you will never enter the kingdom of Heaven" (Matthew 18:3 Cf. Mark 10: 15-16 NJB).

Barbara, who is small, sterile and handicapped without reward, incurs that which the poor incur. The poor are those who are unable to make themselves heard and those whom others consider totally insignificant.

For God on the contrary, the poor are privileged priorities. Thus, He recognizes their unknown worth. According to the Epistle of James:

Did not God choose those who are poor in the eyes of the world, to be rich in faith and heirs of the kingdom he promised to those who love him? Yet you, treated this poor man shamefully. (James 2:5-8).

It is important then, to not sow antipoverty racism but to appreciate Barbara's poverty for what it's worth. First of all, she assumes the poverty upon her quite well- corporeal, psychological and financial. She is "poor in spirit" as Christ invited us to be in the Beatitudes (Matthew 5:1). She has surmounted her handicaps very well and today lives a normal and autonomous life. She has accomplished in this respect, astonishing performances: studies, diplomas, a college degree, religious activities, and radiates in the groups which she animates. She is aided by many friends who recognize her qualities as the Gospel invites them.

The apparitions have aided her in the conquest of her equilibrium. They are a therapeutic factor and not pathological. Let us add that in spite of the depth of her ecstasy, she emerges from it very rapidly, with perfectly normal communication: a humorous smile, human warmth, modesty, attentiveness and adaptation to remarks.

What is most striking is the that she assumes her poverty with paradoxical joy in view of the austerity of her life. Her spontaneous joy, measured and radiant, comes only from God.

Finally, her spiritual life is engaged: She visits the sick in the hospitals, teaches catechism to children in her parish and participates in the prayer group activities on Wednesdays. She belongs to the <u>Legion of Mary</u> and the <u>Third Order Franciscans</u> where she was once elected president. She is active in her parish and the community to which she belongs.

Witness also in her favor:
-her limpidity, and her naivety in the positive sense of the word.
-a total oblivion of self.
-stripped of all ostentation: she is relaxed, welcoming, kind and warm toward her interviewers. She answers only their questions with-

out putting herself in front; without rambling; without talking to herself- a true abandonment to God in all circumstances, good or bad. She has therefore, an authentic supernatural life and this fact bears witness to the authenticity of her ecstatic communication within the control of the relativities stated.

The Conflict and its Solution

The conflict which tied up Barbara's supporters and adversaries became hardened by the fact that it constituted two separate groups: the large group which convened each weekend with Charlie and Carol Nole and the smaller group which supported Barbara. She consequently kept to herself. And this jeopardized a united movement of prayer. But if Barbara abstained from going to the large group, it was to avoid clashes on the part of her adversaries. On the other hand, she regularly attends the parish Rosary where members from the two groups gather on neutral territory. There one does not discuss the apparitions or the project of the cross.

The tension between the two groups is resolving itself (actually without explanation, but by mutual tolerance). Barbara's modesty and discretion during these meetings greatly aids in the solution.

Conclusion

Certainly, the discernment must continue. It will progress but the ecstasy (well tested) and Barbara's edifying life permits the conclusion: *"Blessed are the Poor"*. This conclusion converges with the opinion of Dr. Mark Miravalle, STD, theology professor at the Franciscan University of Steubenville, Ohio, who states:

The reality of Barbara's handicap seems to me to lodge Barbara   in the category of the 'blessed poor and little ones of God,'

who because of an honesty, humility, and innocence that can

come through the purification resulting from exceptional

crosses, makes them all the more suitable instruments for the

transmission of messages from heaven. (Letter of July 20, 1992).

APPENDIX

My Second Visit to Santa Maria (1-2 September 1992)

At Barbara's (September 1st)

Tuesday, September 1, 1992 I made my second investigative trip to Santa Maria. I arrived around five o'clock with Dr. Philippe Loron a neurologist who had also come from Paris (France). We had previously arrived in San Francisco and were driven to Santa Maria by Anna Marie Maagdenberg.

Barbara's home is situated directly across the street from the church. We entered her modest quarters, nicely built in Spanish bungalow style. Barbara lives on the second floor which we reached by an exterior staircase (as in Quebec, to create independence from the renters on each level). The apartment is furnished with thick blue-violet wall to wall carpet. Barbara occupies one bedroom: small, but orderly and well kept with religious statues and pictures.

It is 6 o'clock. Her ecstasy on this day has been taking place since 4:30 P. M. She is kneeing by her bed, very pale, hands joined, facing her corner of prayer.

Up until this time, I had only seen videos of her ecstasies. Seeing her directly says more. Here she is in flesh and bones: petite, short stature, very pale; impressive by her immobility, self effacement, and short hair.

Her face is not expressive: the facial muscles are immobile and droop due to her Turner's Syndrome (and by a reduced operation of certain functions of the cerebral cortex). In fact, during the ecstasy, the drooping corners of her lips give her face a sad appearance. All this would suggest catalepsy, but I soon perceived that she remains perfectly supple. In addition, during certain ecstasies when the Virgin smiles, Barbara normally smiles also. Photographs give evidence of this. Her demeanor is unaffected and uncalculated but with dignity and stature. She is totally in the presence of the invisible person whom she sees and listens to: moreover, completely disconnected.

The ptosis of her eyelids cause them to close about half way. One perceives rare suspicions of blinking but no complete blinks like the frequent blinks of her normal everyday life. We verified this after the ecstasy. Swallowing is rare and slow.

Doctor Loron performed diverse tests:

None of the blinking reflexes exist on advancing his hand toward her eyes. However, the corneal reflex does exists with very minimal reaction, in a precise sense. The reaction to light is very weak (a light in front of her eyes).

The doctor then spreads her arms apart. They automatically return <u>very</u> slowly to their original position, hands joined over the rosary. Her gestures are totally foreign to her conscience.

Jerrie Castro and Anna Marie Maagdenberg (alone with us in the room) try to lift her up but they do not succeed. In spite of her short stature and relative slenderness (barely 100 pounds), she seems heavy like Bernadette at the end of her second apparition: Bernadette's friends were unable to move her, so they had to resort to the strength of Nicolau the miller, who was in the habit of lifting 90 kilo sacks. Another attempt, better prepared with the aid of Dr. Loron, succeeds in lifting Barbara up. After that, the doctor turns her body (trunk) away from the apparition. Her head irresistibly keeps its angle. Her shoulders remain unbalanced as the doctor had placed them but her gaze continues to be fixed toward the same point (toward the apparition). On the other hand, when the doctor attempts to turn her head around there is no more suppleness. The neck muscles resist with all their force and the eyes are riveted toward the same point of the apparition.

Neither is there a reaction when a screen is interposed in front of her eyes: a large screen like that in Medjugorje. The apparition which presents certain characteristics of objectivity, and this includes tactile contacts, is not transmitted by ordinary means (a retinal image on the brain by nerve influx). It is a question of a perception of another order, more immediate from person to person, which takes form in the auditory and visual centers of perception in the brain with adapted muscular response.

The doctor then bends Barbara forward and her head straightens up. During all these last manipulations her legs remain bent; her right knee is forward. She remains for a long time in this uncomfortable position which we had placed her; without any apparent trouble or trembling whatsoever, in spite of maintaining the quasi-acrobatic position of equilibrium.

The doctor measures the physiological rhythms: there are 88 pulsations and 22 respirations per minute. (both in normal limits).

During this ecstasy, the facial muscles remain immobile.

The doctor explores the cutaneous plantar foot reflex by scratching the extremities of her feet with a point of a key. There is no reflex during the ecstasy, while one does exist outside of the ecstasy: another sign of disconnection.

Around 6:30 P. M. the apparition comes to an end in meditation. When Barbara looks at us we are immediately received with a warm smile, and sign of surprise brought about by the change in setting. (We were not present before the apparition began).

She leads us to a small living room situated in the front of the apartment and then leaves us in order to write the message, while kneeing at the foot of her bed.

She answers our questions, notably on the description on the apparition:

The Virgin wore a White veil, a white gown and a golden belt.
She wore no crown. Except, on August 22, the Feast of her Queenship, I did see 12 stars around her head. Her very beautiful eyes are gray blue.

Barbara is very simple, amiable, and warm in a southern style of welcome without pretentiousness.

The Ecstasy of September 2, 1992

The next day September 2, near 4 O'clock Barbara arrives at Jerrie and Bob Castro's where we were staying. She is coming for a reconciliation reunion that evening presided by Monsignor Rohde. But before that she will have her apparition at the usual hour. For this visit, Barbara is prudently dressed: a simple navy blue skirt and white (almost light blue) blouse.

I came into the living room with Dr. Mansour of Los Angeles (UCLA Medical Center) during the second decade of the Rosary, shortly before the beginning of the apparition. Only myself, the two doctors, (Loron and Mansour), Anna Marie Maagdenberg and from time to time our hosts Jerrie and Bob Castro, who were performing hospitality tasks, are there.

It is the same ecstasy as yesterday. The two doctors start the same tests with the same results. Barbara's body is very supple, lending itself to diverse movements impressed on it. They change the axis of her shoulders, but nothing diverts her gaze from its axis. Her body (trunk) does not react to retake its previous position but her neck remains twisted for several minutes. On the other hand, her head resists all change of direction and her gaze does not turn from its axis (toward the apparition). I am more and more surprised by the perfect immobility of Barbara, even in the quasi-acrobatic positions into which the doctors first turned her. The contortions are partly due to her chromosome handicap which in no way restrains her agility. Her movements are rapid, easy and athletic, in all circumstances.

Anna Marie Maagdenberg (stricken by a rash since the day before) comes to pray near Barbara, who takes her hand in order for her to touch the Virgin. Barbara then makes very slight signals that are interpreted to be an invitation to the rest of us present to approach and touch the Virgin also. Barbara guides the hand very gently, without fully opening her eyes (which are half closed), and without looking at the person who is kneeling beside her. She will confirm that she does not see this person. How then does she take their hand? It is the Virgin who guides her. Barbara's explanation agrees perfectly with her behavior at this point.

The evening came to an end by the meeting with Monsignor Rohde. Barbara is there, very discrete and self effacing. The exchange between the opposing groups who avoided heated problems is entirely courteous, fraternal, and positive. It is a step closer toward peace. Barbara contributed toward it.

A few days later, she was at the large annual charismatic conference in Anaheim, California (16,000 people). She attended my workshops at the conference with the same discretion, with which I have never found fault.